KIDS IN CRISIS

KIDS
&
GANGS

Cynthia DiLaura Devore, M.D.

DEDICATION

*To Campbell W. McMillan, for your loving
guidance and gifted instruction.*

Published by Abdo & Daughters, 4940 Viking Drive, Suite 622, Edina, Minnesota 55435.

Library bound edition distributed by Rockbottom Books, Pentagon Tower, P.O. Box 36036, Minneapolis, Minnesota 55435.

Printed in the United States.

Cover Photo credit: Bettmann
Interior Photo credits: Bettmann

Edited By Rosemary Wallner

Devore, Cynthia DiLaura, 1947-
        Kids and Gangs / by Cynthia DiLaura Devore.
            p.   cm. -- (Kids in Crisis)
        Includes bibliographical references and index.
        ISBN 1-56239-323-5
        1. Gangs--United States--Juvenile literature.   [1. Gangs.]
        I. Title.   II. Series.
        HV6439.U5D49   1994
        302.3'4--dc20   94-16821
                                                                CIP
                                                                AC

CONTENTS

1

NOTE TO PARENTS AND TEACHERS

Parents and teachers have an extraordinary task. They must nurture and guide children to become productive, happy adults in a world full of increasing dangers. Drugs and guns are widespread. Violence is glamorized on television and is rampant in the streets. Values are distorted. These are difficult times to be a child. These are also difficult times to be a parent or teacher.

This series is intended to help us keep our children safe in the midst of all this turmoil. The stories and exercises can accomplish this in part by helping young adults develop their own skills at making thoughtful, critical decisions. Each book in the Kids in Crisis series begins with a story (based on a true incident) that illustrates each problem. The story presents children in grades five through seven with a reality-based approach to each topic. The narrative is also meant to be instructional.

The course of decision-making is mapped out as the story unfolds in a step-wise cumulative fashion, building on the choices made by the children in the stories.

In *Kids and Gangs*, the evolution of James from a well-behaved honor student to a gang member parallels the real factors and progression of kids who join gangs. The story takes the reader from the turmoil of James' family and his gradual tagging along with a much admired gang member, his brother, to his experimentation with substances and his alienation from school and eventual joining of the gang. These are all well-documented pre-gang behaviors.

The next chapter discusses choices and consequences, with references to the profile story. This provides an opportunity to discuss alternative choices. It also introduces the concept of impulsive versus thoughtful actions and accountability for choices.

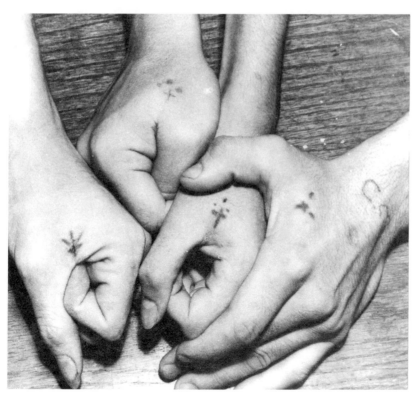

Gang symbols on the hands of these members represent the number of arrests.

The third chapter presents facts and statistics about gangs in a nonjudgmental fashion. This allows the reader to become better informed and thereby better able to develop critical thinking skills.

The next two chapters present the case for and against. Facts are presented so that students can draw their own conclusions.

The sixth chapter returns to the profile story with a look at values that emerged as the incident unfolded.

Finally in "Your Turn," students have their turn to complete projects or think about and discuss issues they have garnered from the book.

Each book in this series should serve as a springboard for discussion between young people and their grownups. Ultimately, the more we communicate with our children at any level, the better equipped they will be to handle life's difficult choices when we may not be around to help them.

Your thoughts and comments on this topic or ideas for future topics are most welcome. The author, like you, is dedicated to the well-being of our children. Please address your comments to the author in care of the publisher.

2

LITTLE EARL'S STORY

The following is based on a true story that happened in South Central Los Angeles in 1990. The gang names and people's names have been changed.

Twelve-year-old James' life had never been easy. For his first five years, he was mostly raised by his older brother, Edward. His parents were not around much. He hardly knew them. His mother died of a drug overdose when he was five. His father, a long-time member of a neighborhood gang called the Rough Rubies, was in prison. He had been convicted of shooting and killing a member of the Black Gates, a rival gang.

James had lived with his grandmother for the past seven years. She was nice, but she was too old to take care of a young boy. Edward was five years older than James and was never around much. He hung around with young members of the Rough Rubies. James' grandmother mostly stayed in the kitchen or watched television. James did not spend much time with her. He did not like what she often said about Edward. His grandmother warned James that Edward was going to wind up in jail like his father. She urged James to go to school and make something good of his life.

James tried. He studied, went to school, and got terrific grades. He even won a scholarship in third grade to attend a summer program at a local college for gifted inner-city students.

His teachers told him that if he continued to study hard, earn good grades, and complete high school, he could win a full college scholarship. His grandmother was proud of him. He was proud of himself, too. For a while, he felt hopeful that he might someday leave his tough neighborhood and be successful. Yet he felt something was missing.

His brother did not like the idea of James attending college. "How can a black boy from the ghetto do anything in a white man's world?" his brother had asked when he heard of the scholarship idea. "You'll be their little puppet, just dancing on a string to their music, man. You want fine clothes like me, you want respect, you join up with me when you're older. Rough Rubies protect their own. Ain't no white man's scholarship gonna protect you. You remember what I said. Grandma's an old lady. She don't know what the real world is like out there. You listen to me."

James adored Edward. He was the closest thing to a father James ever had. In James' eyes, Edward was the picture of success: Edward had lots of friends; wore great clothes, jewelry, and shoes; rode in expensive cars; and dated many girls. James wanted to be like Edward.

From time to time, James began to tag along with Edward. He found out that no one called his brother Edward. His name in the neighborhood, or 'hood as they called it, was Toad. He smiled to think his brother's name was Toad. It sounded cool. On the days that James hung around with Toad's group of friends, or homeboys, James would miss school. It was not a big deal at first. James was so bright, it was easy to make up the work. Yet the more school he missed, the more his grades started to suffer. He began to get into trouble with teachers.

When his teachers tried to talk to him, he rebelled. He felt they did not understand him or his brother.

He was beginning to feel like the only people who understood him were his brothers' friends. He wanted to be a part of their circle.

One day, James skipped school and tagged along with Toad. Toad pulled out a pack of cigarettes and offered James one. "Go on, try one," he said. "You're twelve now, man. I started when I was eight." James did not like the idea of smoking. He hated the smell of cigarette smoke. He knew it caused lung cancer and other horrible stuff. Yet he did not want to disappoint Toad in front of the Rough Rubies. Slowly, he reached for a cigarette. They all laughed at him as he coughed and choked. They patted him on the back. "Your brother is okay," they told Toad. "He ain't afraid to be a man. Maybe someday he'll be a Rough Ruby." James smiled.

At school, the same teachers who used to encourage James now became more and more impatient with his behavior. He was suspended from school for carrying a knife. "This is not like you, James," they said. "You're making the wrong choices. Education is the key. Don't get involved in gangs."

What do they know about me? James thought. They do not know the first thing about who I am or where I am going. They do not respect me. He spent more and more time with members of the gang. With them he felt respected. With them he felt safe. He became distant from his grandmother and teachers. His main ambition now was to make the homeboys proud of him. He wanted to belong to their protected family. He felt ready to ask Toad to help him join the Rough Rubies.

"This ain't no game, boy," Toad told James. "When you is a Ruby, your life belongs to the gang. You gotta be ready to die for them, because they is your family. Nothing else matters. Only the family. Do you understand?"

"I'm ready," James answered as he took a long deep drag off a cigarette. "I'm ready."

With a smile, Toad slapped James across the back. Toad brought James to Big Earl, one of the leaders of the Rough Rubies. He explained to him that James wanted to become a Rough Ruby. Big Earl was an older, hardened gang member. He had scars and tattoos all over his body. He looked over James and did not say a word. He nodded to another gang leader, a guy called Brain Dead. Brain Dead told James to get into the car.

"We'll see if you're ready," said Brain Dead. " We're going on a mission." He watched the three men select guns from a box in the trunk and put them in the car. Brain Dead explained they were going to drive in a GTA and asked James if he knew what it meant. James shook his head. Brain Dead told him it meant Grand Theft Auto. It meant the gang members would be driving in a stolen car. James felt a rush of excitement even though he knew stealing was wrong. He got in the car and rubbed his hands on the expensive leather seats.

In the front seat were Big Earl and a driver called Nutsy. Brain Dead sat in the back with James and did most of the talking. Big Earl just looked around, as if he were searching for someone.

All of a sudden—and for no apparent reason—Big Earl said, "Get 'em!" James heard shots fired and saw two young boys dressed in black jeans, black and yellow jackets, and yellow caps fall to the ground. Big Earl spit out the window. Brain Dead said that the boys were members of the Black Gates and had crossed over onto Rough Rubies turf.

"We protect our 'hood," he explained. James looked out the window, staring at the fallen boys. He nodded to Brain Dead as if he understood.

The car sped off as James heard sirens in the distance. James just sat quietly. He did not know what to say or do, so he just kept quiet. It was wrong to shoot someone. He knew that. Yet he felt very powerful in a car with long-time Rough Rubies with guns. He agreed the 'hood needed protection.

When the car returned to the parking lot where the Rough Rubies had their stronghold, Nutsy, Brain Dead, and even Big Earl smiled at James. "You good, kid," Big Earl said. "You didn't get scared and holler."

Instead of going to school the next day, James went directly to the lot to join his new friends. Big Earl came up to James and handed him a small .22 caliber pistol. He explained they were going on another mission and it was time for James to prove himself worthy of becoming a Rough Ruby. Hitman, another gang member, showed James how to use the gun. They practiced shooting at cans in the parking lot. James felt great power as he pulled the trigger. His blood rushed every time he hit a can. Yes! He smiled.

He got into the car with the same homeboys he had driven with the day before. This time they let James out at the corner, drove a bit, and parked a half block away. They got out to walk toward the same area where they had shot the two boys the day before. James was walking in the opposite direction toward his homeboys, unsure of what was happening. He saw someone dressed in yellow and black, hiding behind a garbage can, and another boy in the same colors behind a thin pole. They had guns. James sensed they were waiting to ambush the Rough Rubies.

Without thinking, he pulled his gun out and fired two shots, one at each of the Black Gates. He hit one. He saw the boy fall. The other boy turned, saw his friend fall and looked with terror at James. The boy ran. James froze. He was so shocked by his own actions he could not move. He stared at the fallen boy.

Brain Dead ran toward James and dragged him toward the car. They got away. Back in the safety of their turf, James was a hero. He had saved three hard-core gang members from certain ambush by a rival gang. Big Earl walked up to James. "You remind me of myself when I was younger," he said. "You royalty, man, and you be known as Little Earl, after me." Big Earl talked like a proud father, and Little Earl felt at last like he had one.

Strangely, Little Earl did not feel sad that he had shot someone. He knew killing was wrong. He thought of his grandmother sitting in church. Yet he felt strong and powerful and oddly at ease. He remembered the fear in the eyes of the young Black Gate who ran away. He laughed as he told the story of the big guy who was afraid of a little twelve-year-old. He did not know if he had killed the Black Gate, but he did not really care.

He had made a good hit and that was all that mattered to him now.

Black Gates were the enemy, and the enemy must die. That was James' new ambition in life. No more thoughts of school or scholarships or college. It was all a joke.

The only reality he knew now was that he was a full-fledged respected member of a family called the Rough Rubies.

The more he got used to carrying a gun, the more he wanted a more powerful weapon. He tried shooting a bigger gun at a dog. Not only did he miss the dog, but the recoil was so strong it threw him to the ground. He decided to use a medium-sized .38 caliber gun. He volunteered whenever there was a mission so he could get more experience.

In two months, Little Earl had his first arrest for assault with a deadly weapon. Because of his age and good school record, he was able to get off with a warning and probation. He continued to have more and more brushes with the law until finally he was connected with the very first shooting. This time there was no getting off, and he was sentenced to four years in juvenile detention.

When he arrived in the detention center the first person he saw was the terrified boy who had escaped from the shooting. This boy was just fourteen and admitted he had been on his first mission, too, that day. The two looked at each other for a few minutes. Then they both started laughing. He introduced himself as Potter, but said his real name was Jerome. He told James that he had been arrested for breaking into houses and stealing for the fourth time.

The judge had been hard on him this time and sentenced him to two years in the detention center.

James found out that Jerome had come from the same kind of family turmoil that James had. He learned that Jerome had been at the same summer program in third grade that James had attended. It was at that moment that James suddenly realized how much he and Jerome had in common. He discovered for the first time that Black Gates are people, regular people, just like him. Jerome was not an enemy. He was a young, bright kid, just like James, who was looking for a sense of family and self-respect. His whole concept of life had been based on a definition of enemy that now seemed silly. He had time, lots of time, in the detention center to rethink just who the enemy is.

3

CHOICES AND CONSEQUENCES

A choice is the act of selecting one thing or behavior over another. A consequence is the outcome or result of the choice made. Every choice has a consequence. Some choices are good, and some consequences are good. Other choices are poor, and the consequences are bad.

James made many choices as he grew up. He began by making the choice to attend school and study. Later, he made the choice to smoke a cigarette even though he knew it could harm him. He decided to miss school to join his brother and hang around with the Rough Rubies. He made this choice even though he knew he had the chance to earn a scholarship to attend college someday.

He chose to get into a stolen car with three known gang leaders carrying guns to go on a mission. Then he accepted his own gun, and used the gun on a rival gang member he had never met. Finally, he chose to become friends with another rival gang member in the detention center.

James' choices are shown in the chart below with the good and bad outcomes of his choices.

JAMES' CHOICES	CONSEQUENCES	
	GOOD OUTCOMES	*BAD OUT-COMES*
1. Attend school	Learn and earn scholarship. Make his grand-mother proud. Get respect of teachers. Earn self-respect. Move to a better life outside the neighborhood. Stay out of trouble with law. Be safe.	Not be outside. Not be a Rough Ruby.
2. Smoke cigarette	Feel grown up. Make Toad proud. Impress Rough Rubies.	Forsake own feelings. Risk illness. Become addicted to nicotine. Have false sense of being grown up. Lose self-respect.
3. Miss school	Time to hang out.	Risk learning. Risk getting in trouble with school and grand-mother and losing their respect.

		Risk losing self-respect. Risk chance for future scholar-ship and college. Risk future chance for life outside of neighborhood.
4. Ride in stolen car with gun-carrying gang members he did not know.	Prove manhood. Experience thrill and excitement. Be accepted into gang.	Risk personal harm by gang members he did not know. Risk arrest and prison for being accomplice to illegal acts. Betray own sense of right and wrong. Risk personal harm by rival gang members Lose self-respect.
5. Shoot Black Gate member.	Become Rough Ruby hero. Save his own new family members.	Risk arrest for murder. Betray own standards and identity for sake of others.

		Develop false sense of manhood. Risk own life. Risk being able to forgive himself. Lose own self-respect.
6. Befriend Jerome.	Have a friend with common problems. Learn about others outside Rough Rubies. Associate with someone who is smart and college material. Build self-respect for following his own mind.	Lose respect of Rough Rubies.

In choices two through five, the risk of the bad outcomes outnumbered the benefits of the good. James, although very bright, may not have considered all the risks of these choices. In some cases, he acted impulsively, without thought. He gave up his own sense of self and his knowledge of right and wrong.

Self-esteem or self-respect is the ability to like yourself. Some experts believe that low self-esteem is a major cause of gang involvement. Children like James who are unhappy, live in dangerous neighborhoods, or have troubled families may not feel worthy of love or respect from others.

Some experts believe these children may seek acceptance by a gang to develop a better sense of self-respect and self-esteem.

In choices two through five, the outcomes shown include abandoning his own set of rules, his code of right and wrong, and his standards of who he was. In each of these choices, one bad outcome was the loss of self-respect. He risked his own identity and values to become one of the gang. If that is true, instead of increasing his self-esteem by joining the gang, he lowered it by not being his own person. Instead of developing self-respect, he risked losing it.

Only in the first and last choices did he follow his own mind. By doing so, he began to rebuild self-esteem. Did joining the gang help James' self-respect or hurt it? The answer to that question is left to James and the reader.

Members of the Vice Lords, Bloods and Crips put their hands together in solidarity at a gang summit in Kansas City.

4

GANG FACTS AND STATISTICS

A gang is a group of people who bond together with common interests, rules, values, and goals, both legal and illegal. People join gangs for social support and entertainment. Some join for economic and financial support. Some gangs are heavily involved in criminal activity, some less so, and some not at all.

Gangs have been in the United States since the early 1900s. For the most part, gangs have been found in large cities among low socio-economic communities. Yet gangs can be found scattered throughout the United States in smaller cities and in some suburban and rural communities. Some gangs are highly organized with smaller chapters springing off the larger group. The most well-known are the Crips and Bloods in Los Angeles, which now have chapters in cities all over the country.

Some gangs are small groups of young people who spend time with each other and think the world is against them. This is a "them against us" way of thinking. That way of thinking often leads to justifying illegal activities. Both large and small gangs can be involved in criminal activities.

Most often, gangs are divided according to racial and ethnic, often minority, communities. Black and Hispanic gangs make up the largest number of gang members.

However, gangs made up of Caucasians, Asians, and immigrants from a variety of small countries are also found throughout the United States. There are also Hybrid gangs whose members include people from different racial and ethnic groups.

Originally, only males made up gangs. Recently, however, female gang membership is increasing. Their level of aggression and violence in some cases has been shown to be worse than their male counterparts. Sometimes girls are regarded as property by the boy gang members. Sometimes they are considered a gangs' turf.

The age range of gang members may be as young as seven or eight and as old as thirty. The average range is between twelve and twenty-two.

Gangs may identify themselves by the clothes, jewelry, and colors they wear. They may claim a part of their neighborhood. They may wear tattoos or self-inflicted scars to identify themselves. They use secret hand signals and symbols. They may also use special words and pictures, called graffiti, painted or written on walls as a way to communicate with each other and other rival gangs.

Different gangs have different reasons for banding together. Some gangs are business organizations created so members can make money. To make money, members may sell drugs. Or they may threaten store owners and force them to pay the gang money for protection. This is known as extortion. They may also promote prostitution, selling sex for money.

Some gangs are concerned mostly with territory rights. According to Community Youth Gang Services, an anti-gang program in South Los Angeles, leadership is passed down from fathers to sons. Many Hispanic gangs are known for wanting territory or "controlling dirt."

A Crips gang member calling himself "Little Monster" tells reporters about the incident leading to the Los Angeles riots.

Some gangs are held together by a strong interest in heavy metal music and drug experimentation. Caucasian gangs, especially The Stoners (known for their long hair and earrings) often take rather than sell drugs.

Other gangs are bonded together by a strong hate for members of other races. The Skinheads, SHARPS, and Boot Boys are gangs who believe in white supremacy. This belief holds that Caucasians are superior to all others. Often, these gangs are responsible for acts of violence against Blacks, homosexuals, and Jews.

Once someone joins a gang, it is very difficult to leave. There is a ritual used by most gangs when someone wants to leave. Three gang members fight the person who wants to leave for three minutes. If the person lives through the fight, he or she can leave. Even then, however, it is not uncommon for the gang or a rival gang to hunt down the person. Someone leaving a gang most often leaves the neighborhood, too.

Law enforcement agencies are finding that more and more gangs are becoming involved in drug selling because of the high profits. The more money or land that is at stake, the greater the risk for violent crimes and murder. The more guns that are available, the greater the risk for murder and more serious injuries.

Gang killings have been on a fairly steady rise since the mid-1970s. Statistics from Community Youth Gang Services, show that in 1977 there were 168 gang killings. In 1992, there were 803. In 1993, there were 719.

In Los Angeles, it is estimated that there are over 100,000 gang members. Between 1973 and 1992, gang fighting in Los Angeles between two rival gangs, the Crips and the Bloods, resulted in over 3,000 deaths. Thousands of people were seriously injured and permanently maimed.

In 1993, the U.S. Department of Justice published *Street Gangs* by Catherine H. Conly. In her book, Conly cited a study by Jeffrey Fagan on gangs in Los Angeles, San Diego, and Chicago. He identified four types of gangs and estimated how gangs were divided:

Social gangs—Had little drug use and little criminal activity. Of all the gangs studied, 28 percent of the gangs were social.

Party gangs—Had extensive drug use and used drug sales to support their own habits. Seven percent of the gangs studied were of this kind.

Serious delinquents— Involved in extensive violent acts and extensive property damage; little drug use or sales. Of the gangs studied, 37 percent were serious delinquents.

Drug gangs—Had extensive drug sales to make money; extensive drug use and organized criminal activity. Of the gangs, 28 percent were drug gangs.

In 1991, during the month of heavy fighting in the Persian Gulf War, 72 Americans were killed. During that same month, 138 were killed on the streets of Los Angeles in gang-related shootings. Some gangs now use a new, seemingly more painful way to pay back a rival. They spare the member, but kill one of his or her family members. Sometimes gang members cripple rivals so they have to live their life in a wheelchair.

5

THE CASE FOR GANGS

Martin Sanchez Jankowski, Ph.D., a sociology professor at the University of California at Berkeley, studied 37 gangs over ten years. He lived with them on the streets. He wrote about his experiences in his book, *Islands in the Street: Gangs and American Urban Society*. He observed that gang members made thoughtful decisions to join gangs as a means to accomplish personal goals. They see a more perfect world on television, for example, and join gangs as one way to claim some improvement in their own lives.

Léon Bing lived with the Crips and Bloods for four years to research her book, *Do or Die*. She found that gangs were like families that provided love for children who did not get it at home. They cared for their injured and raised the young members with more kindness than either group would have received from their homes. She cited many instances where gang members have been supported by the gang financially, even to attend college. Homeless children, neglected by parents, have been taken in and saved by gangs that she observed. These are children who might have died otherwise on the streets.

In Los Angeles, 150 rival gang members listen to Miami Vice star, Edward James Almos, who asked them to put an end to the violence. The gang members spent the evening praying, singing Christmas carols and enjoying a meal together.

George Modica, a former gang member and founder of the Harlem Crips, has since left gang life. However, he recalled he joined for the same reasons others had: He was born into a difficult life and needed security. He was profiled in an article in the November/December 1992 issue of Health magazine. He said gangs give some kids a sense of respect, status, belonging, identity, and pride, especially when these things were not available from family or friends.

T. Rodgers was founder of the original Bloods in Los Angeles in the 1970s. He was an honor student who graduated from high school. He also led a criminal corporation that divided South Central Los Angeles. He dealt in drugs. He was involved in extortion. He was hired to commit murder. The Bloods fought the Crips and T. Rodgers was a major leader. He had been shot and seriously injured four times. He was shot at over 40 times. His own brother, who is now in prison for murder, even shot him. He said that poor children without fathers trying to survive in tough neighborhoods had no place to go for protection except to a gang.

Experts and former gang members generally agree that young people find in gangs the family that the community failed to provide them. If society continues to fall short of giving these young people what they need, can gangs really be condemned for trying to provide for their own?

6

THE CASE AGAINST GANGS

In 1980, Carl Taylor, a professor of criminology at Michigan State University, studied two powerful gangs in Detroit. These gangs operated out of the area where he had been raised as a child, before he went to college on a scholarship. Taylor found that these two gangs were highly organized criminal operations. In an interview in Time magazine in April 1990, he stated that gang members have a distorted view of American values. They want money and respect fast. They will kill in order to get them.

T. Rodgers changed his mind about gangs in the 1990s. After 20 years of being a criminal and training younger people to follow his lead, his conscience began to bother him. He realized the widespread use of the illegal drug crack cocaine had caused gangs to become violent, unreasonable, and dangerous. He finally understood that every crime has a victim. He discovered that many victims are children. He has six children of his own.

In Roselle, N.J., youths inspect a wall covered with drug graffiti. In one year in this neighborhood, the police have arrested 28 crack dealers ranging in age from 12 to 56.

Children often become the victims of gang lifestyle. This photo shows Hispanic children playing amongst garbage strewn in front of a deserted building in Manhattan.

After he left the gang life, Rodgers went into the schools he once terrorized to teach kids about the dangers of gangs. He became a leader in the Amer-I-Can Program. This program's mission is to help hard-core gang members function in the world outside the gang. It encourages gang members to take responsibility for themselves and their actions. It teaches them to stop blaming others, including their parents or society, for their problems.

George Modica, is now paralyzed from a gunshot wound he received from other Crips. Even after being shot, he got back into the gang for a while. Finally, he found his way into a program called Plain Truth Outreach Ministry. He now counsels others like him, wheel-chair-bound from gang shootings, to find a new life away from gangs.

The fact that former hard-core gang founders and members have left the gangs to counsel others away from gangs sends a powerful message. Do gangs really protect their own when they shoot each other? Do gangs take the place of families? Are gangs the only answer?

It is wrong for children to live in homes without proper care. However, is that wrong made right by a young person joining a group that uses violence and drugs and does not let members leave?

7

VALUES

A value is a quality held in high regard by a society. The story of Little Earl is about becoming a gang member and committing violent acts. The story is also about values.

Clearly, Little Earl had a troubled life. His entire family was involved in illegal activities. His grandmother was too old to take care of him. He was on his own without proper supervision. He made some smart choices. However, not surprisingly, he made even more bad choices. Yet even when he made these choices, he remembered basic values that he had been taught by his grandmother and at school. He understood that stealing was wrong. He knew that killing was bad. He felt great pride at his accomplishments in school and his chance for a scholarship to college.

He was able to laugh at himself even when he was in the detention center with a former rival. He came to understand that people are basically the same. He became friends with someone he had tried to kill, someone he had not even known.

He has choices ahead of him in the detention center. He can become more angry and hardened. He can continue to get into trouble with the authorities. However, his time in the detention center might help him to refocus his life. He might learn that he must be accountable for his actions.

He might learn that every choice has a consequence, some good, some bad, and that good choices will make him feel better in the end. Most of all, he might learn that to have the love and respect he craves from others, he must first love and respect himself.

This resident of New York made the choice to set a fire during a riot that was sparked by the police killing of an Hispanic immigrant.

8

YOUR TURN

You've read about one person's struggles with gangs and gang life. You've read some facts about gangs. You've also read basic arguments for and against gangs. Now it's your turn to voice your opinion and start thinking of your own solutions to gangs. Below are some points to think about either alone or in a group. With each point, be creative in your problem solving.

1. Gang experts believe that one reason children join gangs is to find protection. If someone does not feel protected or safe, what could they do to make their lives better and safer? Create a poster listing your ideas. Share your ideas with your class.

2. Another reason children join gangs, experts in gangs believe, is to gain a sense of family love that was lacking at home. They believe poor parenting and a lack of supervision contributes to a child's turning to gangs. Divide a piece of paper into two columns. Label one "Good Parenting" and the other "Poor Parenting." List characteristics you regard as good and bad ways to be a parent. Discuss in a group what you wrote. What kind of a parent do you think you will be?

3. After completing number two, plan a five-day experiment in parenting. Ask each student to bring in something to take care of, such as a five-pound bag of flour, an egg, a small plant, a stuffed animal, or even a large textbook. Pretend the object is your baby. For the next five days, be a parent to your baby. Give it a name.

You do not have to feed it or change diapers, but you must take care of it. Keep it warm and protected. Nurture it with love. Teach it about life as you live it. If you want to go out, take it with you or find a baby-sitter. Each night, write a few sentences about how you took care of your baby. Include the good and bad things you did as a parent.

At the end of five days, review your thoughts about parenting. How would you rate yourself as a parent? Discuss in a group how you felt about yourself as a parent. Was taking care of something hard or easy? Was it fun? Would your baby be at risk for joining a gang? Would your baby have a chance for college or a better life than you may have had?

4. Think about values that are important to you. Think about what values you would want for your children if you were a parent. Discuss in a group how a parent's or older brother's or sister's values and behaviors might affect a child. Discuss how a child without a good role model for values at home may find them elsewhere besides in a gang.

Members of various Los Angeles street gangs hold a press conference to announce a truce in the aftermath of the riots and violence in the city, May 5, 1992. The gang members said they need to unite against the police.

5. Plan a role-playing experiment. Divide your class into three groups. Make one group a powerful gang. Make the second group a weaker gang. Make the third group non-gang members, such as students, store owners, postal workers, and delivery people.

Have each group plan how they want to spend the next 15 minutes. Stage pretend encounters between the two gangs or drug deals between gang and non-gang members. At the end of the 15 minutes, ask everyone to write down how they felt in their role.

Now make the strong gang group the weaker gang group. Make the weaker gang group the non-gang group. Make the non-gang group the strong gang group. Ask each group to plan the next 15 minutes with their new roles. Again have everyone write down how they felt in their second role.

For the last 15 minutes, have the weaker gang group be the non-gang group. Have the non-gang group be the strong gang group. And have the strong gang group become the weaker gang group. After everyone has had a change to role play a third time, have group members write down their feelings.

At the end of the 45 minutes, sit in a large group and share with people how each role made you feel. Focus on issues of power and lack of power and gangsters versus victims.

6. Divide a sheet of paper into two columns. Label one column "Choices" and the other "Consequences." For one week, list choices you make and their consequences. After that week, study the list. Do you see any patterns? Are there more good or bad consequences to decisions you have made over the past week? Think about ways to develop the ability to think critically.

GLOSSARY

Assault: a violent physical or verbal attack. A violent and willful attampt to hurt another.

Extortion: the act or practice of forcefully taking money or property from another.

Gang: a group of persons working to unlawful or antisocial ends.

Homeboy: a slang term referring to a friend or neighbor.

'hood: a slang term referring to one's neighborhood.

Hybrid gang: gangs whose members include people from different racial and ethnic groups.

Probation: the action of suspending the sentence of a conficted offender and giving him freedom during good behavior under the supervision of an officer of a probate court.

Self-esteem: confidence and satisfaction in oneself.

Self-respect: proper respect for oneself as a human being.

Index

For Further Reading

Young Adult books:

•*Gangs* by Renardo Barden, New York, Macmillan, 1989.

Adult books:

•*Coping With Street Gangs* by Margot Webb, New York, Rosen Publishing Group, 1990.

•*Street Gangs: Current Knowledge and Strategies* by Catherine H. Conly, U.S. Department of Justice, August 1993.

ABOUT THE AUTHOR

Dr. Cynthia DiLaura Devore, a pediatrician specializing in school health, is a former special educator and speech pathologist. Her role as a school physician blends her training and experience in both education and medicine. She is the author of Children of Courage, a series of books for children covering issues of loss and separation. It is available through Abdo and Daughters Publishing. Dr. Devore lives in Rochester, New York, with her husband and two sons.